All About Me

Name ....
School ....
Address ....
Phone ....
Email ....
Grade ....
Room ....
School Year ....

Usernames & Passwords

Resources

STUDENTS

Name	Parent/Guardian	Address

Phone/Email	Notes

Happy Birthday

Celebrate!

JANUARY

FEBRUARY

MARCH

APRIL

MAY

JUNE

Holidays &

JULY

4 Independence Day

✦ Park and Recreation Month

AUGUST

9 Book Lovers Day

✦ Get Ready for Kindergarten Month

SEPTEMBER

11 Patriot Day

✦ Labor Day (1st Monday)

✦ Grandparents' Day (Sunday After Labor Day)

✦ Hispanic Heritage Month (Sept. 15–Oct. 15)

✦ Rosh Hashanah (or October)

✦ Yom Kippur (or October)

✦ Native American Day (4th Friday)

OCTOBER

24 United Nations Day

31 Halloween

✦ Columbus Day (2nd Monday)

✦ Fire Prevention Week (2nd Week)

NOVEMBER

1 National Family Literacy Day

11 Veterans Day

✦ Thanksgiving Day (4th Thursday)

✦ Hanukkah (or December)

DECEMBER

25 Christmas Day

26 Kwanzaa Begins

31 New Year's Eve

Special Dates

JANUARY

1 New Year's Day

✦ Martin Luther King, Jr. Day (3rd Monday)

✦ Chinese New Year (or February)

FEBRUARY

2 Groundhog Day

14 Valentine's Day

✦ Black History Month

✦ Presidents' Day (3rd Monday)

MARCH

17 St. Patrick's Day

✦ Women's History Month

✦ Easter (or April)

✦ Passover (or April)

APRIL

1 April Fool's Day

22 Earth Day

✦ National Poetry Month

MAY

1 May Day

5 Cinco de Mayo

✦ Asian-Pacific American Heritage Month

✦ Teacher Appreciation Week (1st Week)

✦ Mother's Day (2nd Sunday)

✦ Memorial Day (Last Monday)

JUNE

14 Flag Day

✦ Pet Appreciation Week (1st Full Week)

✦ Father's Day (3rd Sunday)

✦ National Safety Month

WEEKLY SCHEDULE

Time	Monday	Tuesday	Wednesday	Thursday	Friday

Be Your
Amazing,
Wonderful
Self

JULY

Sunday	Monday	Tuesday	Wednesday

Thursday	Friday	Saturday	Notes

Notes

Expect MORE. They can DO IT!

AUGUST

Sunday	Monday	Tuesday	Wednesday

Thursday	Friday	Saturday	Notes

Notes

Kindness

is taught by

example

SEPTEMBER

Sunday	Monday	Tuesday	Wednesday

Thursday	Friday	Saturday	Notes
			....
			....
			....
			....
			....
			....
			....
			....
			....
			....
			....
			....
			....
			....
			....
			....
			....
			....
			....
			....
			....
			....

Notes

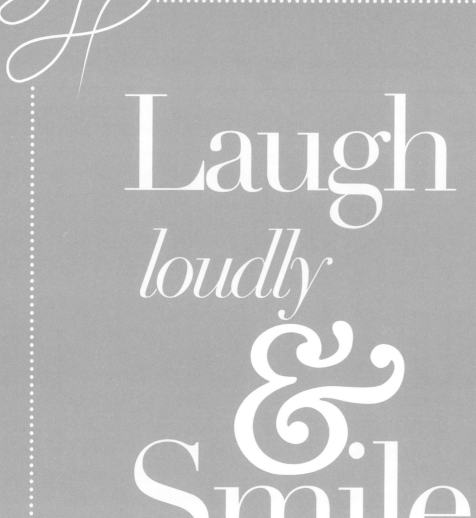

Laugh
loudly
&
Smile
often

OCTOBER

Sunday	Monday	Tuesday	Wednesday

Thursday	Friday	Saturday	Notes

Notes

PERFECTION

is ～～～

not

～～～ *a*

DESTINATION

NOVEMBER

Sunday	Monday	Tuesday	Wednesday

Thursday	Friday	Saturday	Notes

Notes

Silliness
is often
the
solution

DECEMBER

Sunday	Monday	Tuesday	Wednesday

Thursday	Friday	Saturday	Notes

Notes

Take
Risks.
Make
Mistakes.

JANUARY

Sunday	Monday	Tuesday	Wednesday

Thursday	Friday	Saturday	Notes

Notes

TEACHING

is

YOUR
SUPERPOWER

FEBRUARY

Sunday	Monday	Tuesday	Wednesday

Thursday	Friday	Saturday	Notes
			....
			....
			....
			....
			....
			....
			....

Notes

To them,
YOU
····· are ·····
PERFECT

MARCH

Sunday	Monday	Tuesday	Wednesday

Thursday	Friday	Saturday	Notes
			....
			....
			....
			....
			....
			....
			....

Notes

When
IN DOUBT,
dance
it
out

APRIL

Sunday	Monday	Tuesday	Wednesday

Thursday	Friday	Saturday	Notes

Notes

You
are
everything
to
SOMEONE

MAY

Sunday	Monday	Tuesday	Wednesday

Thursday	Friday	Saturday	Notes
			....
			....
			....
			....
			....
			....
			....
			....
			....
			....
			....
			....
			....
			....
			....
			....
			....
			....
			....
			....
			....
			....
			....
			....

Notes

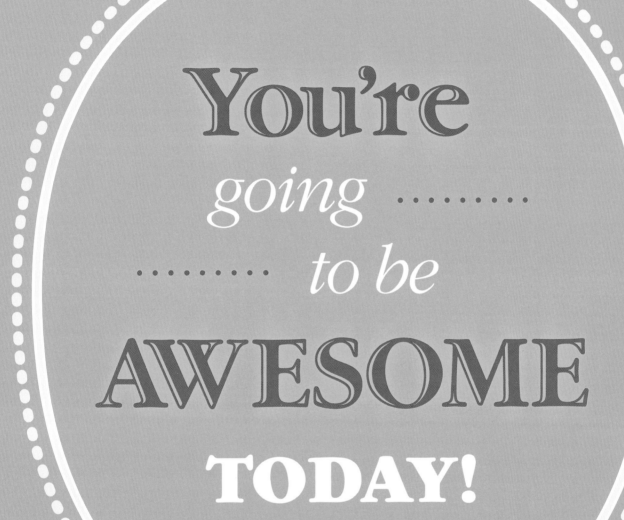

You're
going ....
.... *to be*
AWESOME
TODAY!

JUNE

Sunday	Monday	Tuesday	Wednesday

Thursday	Friday	Saturday	Notes
			....
			....
			....
			....
			....
			....
			....
			....
			....
			....
			....
			....
			....
			....
			....
			....
			....
			....
			....
			....
			....
			....
			....
			....

Notes

You've
got
THIS

Week #	Time:	Time:	Time:
	Subject:	Subject:	Subject:

Monday

/

Tuesday

/

Wednesday

/

Thursday

/

Friday

/

Subject: Subject: Subject:

Time:	Time:	Time:	Time:
Subject:	Subject:	Subject:	Subject:

Week #	Time:	Time:	Time:
	Subject:	Subject:	Subject:

Monday

/

Tuesday

/

Wednesday

/

Thursday

/

Friday

/

Subject: Subject: Subject:

Time:	Time:	Time:	Time:
Subject:	Subject:	Subject:	Subject:

Week #	Time:	Time:	Time:
	Subject:	Subject:	Subject:

Monday

/

Tuesday

/

Wednesday

/

Thursday

/

Friday

/

Time:

Subject:

Time:	Time:	Time:	Time:
Subject:	Subject:	Subject:	Subject:

Week #	Time:	Time:	Time:
	Subject:	Subject:	Subject:

Monday

/

Tuesday

/

Wednesday

/

Thursday

/

Friday

/

| Time: | Time: | Time: | Time: |
| Subject: | Subject: | Subject: | Subject: |

Week #	Time:	Time:	Time:
	Subject:	Subject:	Subject:

Monday

/

Tuesday

/

Wednesday

/

Thursday

/

Friday

/

	Time:	Time:	Time:
	Subject:	Subject:	Subject:

Time:

Subject:

Time:

Subject:

Time:

Subject:

Time:

Subject:

Week #	Time:	Time:	Time:
	Subject:	Subject:	Subject:

Monday

/

Tuesday

/

Wednesday

/

Thursday

/

Friday

/

Time:

Subject:

Time:

Subject:

Time:

Subject:

Time:

Subject:

Week #	Time:	Time:	Time:
	Subject:	Subject:	Subject:

Monday

/

Tuesday

/

Wednesday

/

Thursday

/

Friday

/

Time:	Time:	Time:	Time:
Subject:	Subject:	Subject:	Subject:

Week #	Time:	Time:	Time:
	Subject:	Subject:	Subject:

Monday

/

Tuesday

/

Wednesday

/

Thursday

/

Friday

/

Subject: Subject: Subject:

Time:	Time:	Time:	Time:
Subject:	Subject:	Subject:	Subject:

Week #	Time:	Time:	Time:
	Subject:	Subject:	Subject:

Monday

/

Tuesday

/

Wednesday

/

Thursday

/

Friday

/

Subject: | Subject: | Subject:

Time:	Time:	Time:	Time:
Subject:	Subject:	Subject:	Subject:

Week #	Time:	Time:	Time:
	Subject:	Subject:	Subject:

Monday

/

Tuesday

/

Wednesday

/

Thursday

/

Friday

/

Subject: Subject: Subject:

Time:	Time:	Time:	Time:
Subject:	Subject:	Subject:	Subject:

Week #	Time:	Time:	Time:
	Subject:	Subject:	Subject:

Monday

/

Tuesday

/

Wednesday

/

Thursday

/

Friday

/

Time:

Subject:

Time:

Subject:

Time:

Subject:

Time:

Subject:

Week #	Time:	Time:	Time:
	Subject:	Subject:	Subject:

Monday

/

Tuesday

/

Wednesday

/

Thursday

/

Friday

/

Time:	Time:	Time:	Time:
Subject:	Subject:	Subject:	Subject:

Week #	Time:	Time:	Time:
	Subject:	Subject:	Subject:

Monday

/

Tuesday

/

Wednesday

/

Thursday

/

Friday

/

Time: Subject: Subject: Subject:

Time:	Time:	Time:	Time:
Subject:	Subject:	Subject:	Subject:

Week #	Time:	Time:	Time:
	Subject:	Subject:	Subject:

Monday

/

Tuesday

/

Wednesday

/

Thursday

/

Friday

/

Time:	Time:	Time:	Time:
Subject:	Subject:	Subject:	Subject:

Week #	Time:	Time:	Time:
	Subject:	Subject:	Subject:

Monday

/

Tuesday

/

Wednesday

/

Thursday

/

Friday

/

Time:	Time:	Time:	Time:
Subject:	Subject:	Subject:	Subject:

Week #	Time:	Time:	Time:
	Subject:	Subject:	Subject:

Monday

/

Tuesday

/

Wednesday

/

Thursday

/

Friday

/

Time:	Time:	Time:	Time:
Subject:	Subject:	Subject:	Subject:

Week #	Time:	Time:	Time:
	Subject:	Subject:	Subject:

Monday

/

Tuesday

/

Wednesday

/

Thursday

/

Friday

/

Subject: | Subject: | Subject:

Time:	Time:	Time:	Time:
Subject:	Subject:	Subject:	Subject:

Week #	Time:	Time:	Time:
	Subject:	Subject:	Subject:

Monday

/

Tuesday

/

Wednesday

/

Thursday

/

Friday

/

Time:

Subject:

Time:	Time:	Time:	Time:
Subject:	Subject:	Subject:	Subject:

Week #	Time:	Time:	Time:
	Subject:	Subject:	Subject:

Monday

/

Tuesday

/

Wednesday

/

Thursday

/

Friday

/

Time:	Time:	Time:	Time:
Subject:	Subject:	Subject:	Subject:

Week #	Time:	Time:	Time:
	Subject:	Subject:	Subject:

Monday

/

Tuesday

/

Wednesday

/

Thursday

/

Friday

/

| Time: | Time: | Time: | Time: |
| Subject: | Subject: | Subject: | Subject: |

Week #	Time:	Time:	Time:
	Subject:	Subject:	Subject:

Monday

/

Tuesday

/

Wednesday

/

Thursday

/

Friday

/

Time:	Time:	Time:	Time:
Subject:	Subject:	Subject:	Subject:

Week #	Time:	Time:	Time:
	Subject:	Subject:	Subject:

Monday

/

Tuesday

/

Wednesday

/

Thursday

/

Friday

/

Time:	Time:	Time:	Time:
Subject:	Subject:	Subject:	Subject:

Week #	Time:	Time:	Time:
	Subject:	Subject:	Subject:

Monday

/

Tuesday

/

Wednesday

/

Thursday

/

Friday

/

| Time: | Time: | Time: | Time: |
| Subject: | Subject: | Subject: | Subject: |

Week #	Time:	Time:	Time:
	Subject:	Subject:	Subject:

Monday

/

Tuesday

/

Wednesday

/

Thursday

/

Friday

/

Subject: Subject: Subject:

Time:	Time:	Time:	Time:
Subject:	Subject:	Subject:	Subject:

Week #	Time:	Time:	Time:
	Subject:	Subject:	Subject:

Monday

/

Tuesday

/

Wednesday

/

Thursday

/

Friday

/

	Subject:	Subject:	Subject:

Time:	Time:	Time:	Time:
Subject:	Subject:	Subject:	Subject:

Week #	Time:	Time:	Time:
	Subject:	Subject:	Subject:

Monday

/

Tuesday

/

Wednesday

/

Thursday

/

Friday

/

Subject: Subject: Subject:

Time:

Subject:

Time:

Subject:

Time:

Subject:

Time:

Subject:

Week #	Time:	Time:	Time:
	Subject:	Subject:	Subject:

Monday

/

Tuesday

/

Wednesday

/

Thursday

/

Friday

/

Time:

Subject:

Time:	Time:	Time:	Time:
Subject:	Subject:	Subject:	Subject:

Week #	Time: Subject:	Time: Subject:	Time: Subject:

Monday

/

....
....
....
....
....
....

Tuesday

/

....
....
....
....
....
....

Wednesday

/

....
....
....
....
....

Thursday

/

....
....
....
....
....
....

Friday

/

....
....
....
....
....

Time:

Subject:

Time:

Subject:

Time:

Subject:

Time:

Subject:

Week #	Time:	Time:	Time:
	Subject:	Subject:	Subject:

Monday

/

Tuesday

/

Wednesday

/

Thursday

/

Friday

/

Time:

Subject:

Time:

Subject:

Time:

Subject:

Time:

Subject:

Week #	Time:	Time:	Time:
	Subject:	Subject:	Subject:

Monday

/

Tuesday

/

Wednesday

/

Thursday

/

Friday

/

Time:	Time:	Time:	Time:
Subject:	Subject:	Subject:	Subject:

Week #	Time:	Time:	Time:
	Subject:	Subject:	Subject:

Monday

/

Tuesday

/

Wednesday

/

Thursday

/

Friday

/

Time:

Subject:

Time:

Subject:

Time:

Subject:

Time:

Subject:

Week #	Time:	Time:	Time:
	Subject:	Subject:	Subject:

Monday

/

Tuesday

/

Wednesday

/

Thursday

/

Friday

/

Time:	Time:	Time:	Time:
Subject:	Subject:	Subject:	Subject:

Week #	Time:	Time:	Time:
	Subject:	Subject:	Subject:

Monday

/

Tuesday

/

Wednesday

/

Thursday

/

Friday

/

Time:	Time:	Time:	Time:
Subject:	Subject:	Subject:	Subject:

....
....
....
....
....
....

....
....
....
....
....
....

....
....
....
....
....
....

....
....
....
....
....
....

....
....
....
....
....
Subject: Subject: Subject: Subject:

Week #	Time:	Time:	Time:
	Subject:	Subject:	Subject:

Monday

/

Tuesday

/

Wednesday

/

Thursday

/

Friday

/

Time: Time: Time:

Subject: Subject: Subject:

Time:

Subject:

Time:

Subject:

Time:

Subject:

Time:

Subject:

Week #	Time:	Time:	Time:
	Subject:	Subject:	Subject:

Monday

/

Tuesday

/

Wednesday

/

Thursday

/

Friday

/

Time:

Time:

Time:

Subject:

Subject:

Subject:

Time:	Time:	Time:	Time:
Subject:	Subject:	Subject:	Subject:

Week #	Time:	Time:	Time:
	Subject:	Subject:	Subject:

Monday

/

Tuesday

/

Wednesday

/

Thursday

/

Friday

/

Time:	Time:	Time:	Time:
Subject:	Subject:	Subject:	Subject:

Week #	Time:	Time:	Time:
	Subject:	Subject:	Subject:

Monday

/

Tuesday

/

Wednesday

/

Thursday

/

Friday

/

Time:

Time:

Time:

Subject:

Subject:

Subject:

Time:	Time:	Time:	Time:
Subject:	Subject:	Subject:	Subject:

Week #	Time: Subject:	Time: Subject:	Time: Subject:

Monday

/

Tuesday

/

Wednesday

/

Thursday

/

Friday

/

Time:	Time:	Time:	Time:
Subject:	Subject:	Subject:	Subject:

Week #	Time:	Time:	Time:
	Subject:	Subject:	Subject:

Monday

/

Tuesday

/

Wednesday

/

Thursday

/

Friday

/

Time:	Time:	Time:	Time:
Subject:	Subject:	Subject:	Subject:

Week #	Time:	Time:	Time:
	Subject:	Subject:	Subject:

Monday

/

Tuesday

/

Wednesday

/

Thursday

/

Friday

/

Subject: Subject: Subject:

Time:	Time:	Time:	Time:
Subject:	Subject:	Subject:	Subject:

Week #	Time:	Time:	Time:
	Subject:	Subject:	Subject:

Monday

/

Tuesday

/

Wednesday

/

Thursday

/

Friday

/

Subject: Subject: Subject:

Time:	Time:	Time:	Time:
Subject:	Subject:	Subject:	Subject:

Notes

Design by Linda Rubes and Nilou Safavieh